MOTHER MUSE

Caribbean poet Lorna Goodison
was born in Kingston, Jamaica.
She was appointed Poet Laureate
of Jamaica in 2017. In 2018, she
received a Windham-Campbell
Literature Prize, and in 2019 she
was awarded the Queen's Gold
Medal for Poetry.

MOTHER MUSE

Lorna Goodison

CARCANET POETRY

First published in Great Britain in 2021 by
Carcanet
Alliance House, 30 Cross Street
Manchester, M2 7AQ
www.carcanet.co.uk

A CIP catalogue record for this book is
available from the British Library.

ISBN 978 1 80017 106 0

Book design by Andrew Latimer
Printed in Great Britain by SRP Ltd, Exeter, Devon

The publisher acknowledges financial
assistance from Arts Council England.

CONTENTS

To Margaret Busby and Dawn Davis,
wayfinders in the world of publishing,
and in memory of filmmaker
Jan Sharp, who believed.

MOTHER MUSE

Keep doing the island's housekeeping.
Scour and rinse out the mouth of a river,
plastic scandal-bag clogged.

You're a pin-up girl in a one-piece bathing suit
I saw you sew yourself; it is ruched and tucked
like a washboard across your belly.

Your wet let-out hair cascades down your back.
You dive in and breaststroke the familiar
long-lap river rushing past

your old childhood home all but gone to ruin;
captured by pirate cousin. You backstroke,
float and butterfly into Lucea Harbour

where I'd left you in the Bardo days after death.
I'd clung to your capable hand losing warmth
as we travelled to the Western shore.

You stepped into the deep and embraced big sea
waves; turned to me back on land and said,
'You cannot come with me yet'.

Then off you swam. I set off for home, feet barely
touching ground till I reached Constant Spring;
where I lifted my eyes to the hills.

Go long you said, I'll be muse, you be yourself.

NEW YEAR'S MORNING 1965

Out of the mesh mouth radio the news strains at dawn:
He'd killed her and surrendered to the Rockfort police.

Recall this: some said she was wild woman; fair game
for one straight blade to the heart.

You stayed in bed and wept. Common knowledge:
His light was inclined to combust into violence.

For his unburied birth caul shaded him, made the slide
stick and drive him to madhouse. Cramp and paralyze him.

Times he broke free, his horn work outshone Gabriel's.

Alumnus of Alpha Boys School for the wayward, his mother
handed him over to Sister Mary Ignatius, nun more deserving

of a T.V. show than the high flying one of starched cornette;
she was a devotee of rhythm and blues, jazz, bebop

and all other worldly music. Athlete and able coach of cricket,
boxing, football, netball, and table tennis.

Sister Iggy, as deejay, played the speeches of Malcolm X
for young Black men she helped master musical instruments.

Hail Iggy's students taking our own home-grown music
all over the known world! She loved Don like her own.

Thinned rosary beads petitioning for his peace;

and for Anita 'Margarita' Mahfouz second-generation
daughter of Lebanon, gorgeous Bohemian, Alpha woman,

blessed and cursed with nurse spirit; she, a fellow traveler
with worthy women devotees of Love without borders,

was billed most times as *a rhumba dancer*. Few discerned
how her steps retraced desert routes of camel trains.

One night you caught her act at the Ad Astra, but had no words
in those days to describe her.

The atoms in that smoky place on Windward Road stirred
sands storm that caused wine bibbers to weep into rum cups.

And all in these poems would have come under the influence
of Rastafari 'The Earth Most Strangest (Wo)man'.

Thus spoke Ras Kumi.

And these words are offered in thanks to those who started flames
that consumed them as they blazed trails so we are now free to be:

musicians, dancers, thinkers, writers, artists, mystics.

THE NEAR NOONDAY DANCE OF SISTER IGGY

When Sister Ignatius performs her near noonday dance,
the swing skirts of her long habit polish her ankles.
'Veni sancti spiritus' she intones till paraclete
manifests, enfolds her in winged arms; they waltz.

Unseen yet ever near, sweet spirit turns in key holes,
pours concrete walls, limbos under barred windows.
She knows not how, but their lock-step kickstarts
alleluia, alleluias tumbling through breeze blocks.

Spirit inquires, 'Dear Sister, how are our charges'
'You mean our boys lost, abandoned, wayward?
Doing well. They carry the good news of our home
grown music to audiences all over the known world.

They have been found, give thanks, by music's grace.
Our Alpha musicians are now musical ambassadors!'
Divine presence allows, 'O Mary Ignatius, well done',
air kisses her on the brow; she finds herself alone.

Sister Iggy clasps her hands. Sister Iggy bows her head.
The bell sounds for noon prayers; hers have been said.

SUGAR

Perfumed by sugar's money musk, her newly refined
ancestors took upon themselves airs of mount plenty.
Aromatic sweet canes render bitter waters potable.

Cane's cultivators—the millions of stolen Africans
counted by Massa as less-than; and the young Mary
was raised not to follow their ways or consider them

playmates. 'For you and them are not companion'.
But the girl was alive and quick to her people's music.
Shivered her feet to burru drums, sheltered wild notes

escaped from blackbird work gangs, marked converter
call to score new beats drummed into barrel staves
the one-drop way. She made moan to sorrow songs—

belly-band of what hard labour breaks. O the dig and
plant and weed and cut and juice and boil, blood and
toil required for brute cane to achieve sweet mouth,
out of which would come our music.

A ROSE FROM SAINT THERESE

O little Therese of the child Jesus, pick for me a rose
from the heavenly gardens and send it to me
as a message of Love.
Novena Prayer Card

Did Mary kiss the cool roseate plastic face and pray
for the teenaged saint to come bearing the rose herself?

Did that kiss start her request to find her own patron saint?
Did Therese manifest in response to Mary's request,

flown to France and through the garden gates at Lisieux
convent where the way of the little flower flourished?

Would she recognize her if she was ringed by a rose scent?
So none of her school girl friends passed the fragrance test?

Is that why Mary played with the boys till she beat them
at every sport to become limber-limb, slender, athletic

girl, light on her feet, quick to step to the world's music?
At sixteen did she hear a voice call her on the playing field?

Was her vision lit up by pepper lights sparking round her feet?
String of lights she kicked against—walking brisk brisk

with head held down; did she observe how the commonest
flower is drip-fed rain and nourished with sun hot food?

Those would not have been the roses she'd prayed for.
Did she decide to accept them as a token from the little flower?

The splendor of the rose, the whiteness of the lily,
do not rob the little violet of its scent...

Tapta nap ta nap ta na na,went the wind in the cane reeds;
in the ground cover flowers she heard stir a new music.

No force-up scarlet hibiscus fanning into flame of the forest.
Absence of red ants in abundance, so at a glance one would
mistake that swarm for burning bush.

Disembodied voice did not command, remove shoes and stand,
ten toes spread on holy ground; no nocturnal name call
to answer with, 'Speak Lord thy servant heareth.'

This came at noon on the school playground where she'd shied
a ball so hard that the wicket split, outing the batsman
and her side won.

The voice said: Clean bowled! Well done, my own Mary!'

Thus spoke the Divine commentator to teenager Mary Davies
who was all set to go off to play ball (or rock around the clock
in the world's dance hall).

Said she: 'You don't know any girls who are not named Mary?'

I am the girlchild who can play football, cricket, netball
and table tennis. Featherweight, I box. I could be deejay
who makes the crowd swing; that is the Mary I am.

I want to marry you and make you the mother to scores
of boys who'll go wide of the mark if I do not give you
charge of raggamuffins this world would write off.

Youths I have appointed my very own musical co-creators.
'Say yes, say yes,' the waiting Alpha boys chorused.
From henceforth you will be called after St Ignatius
'Bless up, bless up!' Alpha boys chorus. Bless our sister Iggy.

THE CALL—MARY'S VERSION

My mother ascends a ladder of light up to the clouds.
She is dressed in a lacy cloud-white wedding gown.
In childhood this was my dream.

My relatives told me that my mother went home
to live with Jesus when I asked why she'd leave
me behind to grow with others.

I was raised by my dutiful aunt who cared for me,
but still and all, all my life, I'd miss my mother,
whom I'm sure would have kissed my face,

and hushed my cries when she untangled my hair
and brushed it smooth. She'd hum a charming tune
when she steam-pressed my school uniform,

and the knife pleats would lie flat; she'd remark
how I'd grown as she lotioned my limbs, she would
make me polish my shoes. She'd be strict.

I lived in dream state, only coming fully awake
out there on the school playing fields where I
developed into all-round athlete who one day hit

a cricket ball for six so it flew the high wire fence
and landed in the yard of the school for bad boys.
I went to retrieve it and met with that little band

some others would dismiss as waifs and strays.
Just little ones really; poor boy pickney with whom
I made friends. They so in need of mothering

I myself always wanted. So I left my aunt's house
at age seventeen; I am going to be a bride of Christ
said I, I intend to take care of His children.

I will take the name of St Ignatius who believed
God is found everywhere in everything. You will
not last one weekend inside that nunnery, she said

and handed me a thin silver sixpence for my bus fare
back to Innswood. Just in case.

SISTER IGGY THINKS OF JESSI RIPOLE

They say Portugal is lovely this time of year.
The roofs are clay red and bougainvillea
studies new ways to shimmy and cascade

across tiles and wide wrought iron balconies,
hung over with last night's damp bed linen,
on display as sweat-stained tapestries.

And the sea is a deep dish, silver with sardines,
and long meter waves wash songs of sailors
back to shore as mournas, fado, mournas.

And I think of creole Jessi Ripole who'd heard
all her life of lovely Lisboa, city of her fathers,
and could have used her inheritance

to fill a wicker trunk with picotted linen dresses,
and set sail like some in reverse Columbus;
landing in Porto de Lisboa as lady of substance.

Good Jessi who suffered the little children to come
into the place bought with four hundred pounds
plus. Forty-three acres on South Camp road,

become refuge and safe home for those dispersed
strayaway gangs, offspring of the ex-enslaved
turned loose to wild without fence or friend.

Josephine Ximinez and Louise Dugiol—blessed!
for joining with Jessi to start up a new world.
In the beginning, a cottage with one orphan girl...

WHAT SISTER IGGY SAW

Rambunctious, rowdy, rompers who carouse,
and never speak when they can bawl out loud.
Prefer run-fast to walk, and stretch fingers
to quick pick fight, and slingshot or fling stone.
She saw possibilities in boy form.
And when each one found his destined calling
he'd channel heartfelt through his medium
of musical instrument; crying out
to lost loved ones. Ripped from kin connections
their blow-for-breath made them master laments.
Alpha boys personified resilience.
They created music. Music made them.
What Iggy saw were not wayward boys,
just potential energy she'd harness.

THE ALPHA BOYS AT VESPERS

At the evening hour
of vespers
O mother dear
remember me.
Mother whose own
firstborn
was dispatched
to earth
on life-save errand.

O mother
from your throne
look down upon
we the ones you gave
this gift of music
and keep us,
keep us in safekeeping.

Pipe boys
like fine-boned
sparrows
that trill and trill.
Voices break into deep,
then deeper still
petitioning
guardian mother
to keep watch as they sleep.

Outside the boys home
hard-life's work worn
women and men—
neighbourhood
standing-room-
-only audience,
assemble to be
hushed by hymns.
Quieted by canticles.

BOXING LESSONS WITH SISTER IGGY

I play for you the speeches of a man born Malcolm Little,
alias Detroit Red; reborn as Malcolm X, whose sainted
mother Louise, was native of Grenada, island of nutmeg.

I pray for you, but keep in mind the words of the Teacher:
'I send you out into the world as sheep amidst wolves,
be wise as serpents and guiless as doves'.

I practice with you young Alpha men the fine art of self
defense, I lace up tight my *Everlast* boxing gloves,
I juke, jab, and feint the straight across left hook.

I am penpals with Sugar Ray Robinson; it is through
our correspondence course that he instructs me in these
pugilistic arts that I myself am now able to teach you.

I preach vigilance—the enemy can appear as wolf or viper
music might charm—play your horn. But should you need
to chuck him off, I instruct you boys how to box.

SISTER IGGY DEEJAY

She is no whistling woman; but she warbles
as she sits perched at her desk to compile
the playlist for Saturday afternoon dances
where she's operator of Mutt and Jeff
sound system.

Instruments of brass range row on row
on wooden shelves planed by apprentices.
She has dispatched two of the Alpha boys
to Times Store to buy hot 45's heard on radio.

Her chatter between platters will range wide.
Here, she will say, you'll hear, Amos Milburn
singing, 'One Scotch, One Bourbon One Beer'.
You boys must not imitate his inebriated ways.

Enjoy this blues just the same.
Next I'll play piano concerto #21 by Mozart
—a boy genius. So she spins, she enlightens.
Later under tutelage of bandmasters:

Rueben Delgado, Lennie Hibbert and Sparrow
Martin, the boys will grasp what they've learned
then bend familiar sounds till they
become new again.

She helped to make them into men who make
music that will save them.

SISTER IGGY SPEAKS OF DONALD

I'm aware that in accordance with the rules of our order,
the ground is level where we stand equal in the eyes
of our author and finisher who shows no partiality.

But I cannot in all good conscience deny that I did err
oftentimes on the side of showing favor to Donald;
the child I might have had if I'd married a mortal

man instead of the Christ I wed in the great cathedral,
accepting his ring along with seven other brides of his,
gowned and veiled in white garments of lace and net;

our wedding night spent in chaste and narrow beds.
If I had married a young man from St Georges College
then I might have birthed a boy like the one brought

here by his mother Doris, because ordinary school walls
could not hold him. Earthly authorities call it truancy,
but my sense is his was a soul in search of a place

to make itself through music. He was music made
manifest as Don Drummond   Don D   Don Cosmic.
I called him my own Donald. He made the trombone

weep or rejoice like a human voice; superabundantly
gifted he was, but such genius is magnet to demonic
spiteful spirits. His was deep melancholia inclined

to flare up into violence. I prayed, said novenas,
dedicated decade after decade of rosaries, yet still
he met his fate in the person of an extraordinary

woman who came from the east and rose upon him
like the sun. I prefer not to speak of how it went down.
I pray they are both at peace.

I beg you judge him by his music.

THE POET AND MARGARITA

Except for that bone
handled knife,
bullseye in your chest,
your skin is unblemished.
You have stayed the same
in every photograph—woman a glow

How did you find your way
to where I live now?

The number 12 bus
I rode to go home
stopped along
Windward Road
where I once saw
you and Marcia Griffiths
at the bus stop.

The two of you:
luminous.

No disrespect my sistren
I do not want to write
about you.
I'm done with your tragic
woman story.

But you just tilt
your head to one side,
flash that Photoplay
smile, and say
it's because you are
so easy to cry
I want you
to tell them
for me.

MARGARITA'S VERSION

Our name Mahfouz means one who is well protected;
and my father Jad Eid tried his mad complicated best
to gather we his daughters like bright fish into nets.
See this studio portrait of him and his four daughters?
We are well-dressed; he was a damaged, not a broke man.

My mother is not in this picture; she was born a Virtue
who knew poems by heart; and one day careened under
the wheels of a moving vehicle—another tragic woman
in a story. When my father's fish emporium burned
down, unprotected he lamented he'd not sired strong sons.

I was ripped from my family picture by the dark destroyer.
I sewed myself a pink cocktail-length *peau de soi* dress,
took his gold band from a justice of the peace, gave him
children, and became battered wife who could not love
a man who used me as flesh and blood punching bag.

They call me rhumba dancer. I do not know what that
means. I ask that you tell them for me how my father
brought with him from Lebanon a load of old hymns
he'd chant when sorrow washed a grey oily sea over
our family life, and violence dismantled our house.

My Father called upon the ninety-nine names of God.
The One. The Healer. The Compassionate. The Merciful...
I committed them all to memory, stored them within
till some presence began to arrange my limbs; a force
lifted and set down my feet, tilted my hips. Guided.

They say I taught myself; but I was led to the way of wild
women who sacrifice themselves for love, like the partridge
who for love of the moon, swallows glowing hot coals.
And when my Ungu Malungu man split open my chest
his own was inscribed next to the ninety-nine names.

THE FISHERMAN CANNOT SING OF THE CEDARS OF LEBANON

Father our father sing to us your daughters,
sing of the cedars of Lebanon fought over
by men and demi-gods. Cedars with roots

that stretch down into deep waters, grow up
to panel the temple walls of Kings David
and Solomon, secrete embalming resin

for Egyptians and supply papyrus for scrolls.
Material of mighty ships and railroad tracks.
Aromatic Cedars that grow in Kadisha valley

beneath Lebanon's long mountain shadows.
My daughters, I have never been to the valley
of Kadisha. I was born by the Mediterranean

and my forefathers fished the long coastline
in small boats with no sails. I have ventured far
from the shores of my homeland, I have come

seeking my fortune in the turquoise waters
of the Caribbean. On some quiet starry nights
out at sea, I have heard remembered melodies

being played upon oud and nay, and my heart
breaks like a wave on the shores of Lime Cay.
O my daughters, both seas swell within me.

Where they converge foam storm and rage.
For I wanted muscular man children to aid
and assist me, my own boys I could teach

ancient ways to harvest the sea, my youth men
who'd grow tall and substantial as God's trees.
Your mother bore me no sons. I'm doomed

to dwell in a house of women, all soft bodies
ruled by the moon. I bring the wrath of sea
storms home. No, I cannot sing of cedars.

Mother was born a Virtue. She was mild-mannered, she was soft
spoken; she would have made a good wife for a school-teacher
or a parson who loved books.

They could have sat down side by side on a spacious verandah
and read to each other. When a breeze would come wafting up
from the seaside to stir her skirts,

they would have quoted from Shelley's Ode to the West Wind,
and Christina Rossetti who enquired, Who has seen the wind?
Their nights would be tender, their days sweet.

She would recite verses to her four daughters, mostly Romantic
poetry about daffodils and flowers they had never seen. Her name
was Brenda May, she was drawn to tragic heroines.

Ophelia in her garland of crow-flower, nettles, daysies and long
purple, long purple, drowned in a weedy river as she chanted
snatches of tearup tunes.

Anna, unhappy wife and mother who ended up beneath train
wheels. Her mother loved poetry. She married a wild man
from Lebanon who loved the sea.

Where he touched her he left fish scales like errant sequins.

A PRAISE FOR MARGARITA ANITA

Her fragrant presence could have won her the Star's
Miss Apple Blossom contest; she fell hard instead,
for a genius she accompanied to recording studios.

His name itself was riddim: Don Drummond, Don D,
Don Man of mind split to hold his gift: Don master
of the eerily eloquent slide trombone.

Don of sorrows born to catch and release one people's
hurt from a horn's cup. Don Cosmic the astronomer
who scored the sphere's music with indelible pencil stub.

It is written how Margarita Anita was a dancer in the club
and that she lost her children and home when doomed
love set its seal upon her and her beloved.

O Margarita Mahfood and Don Drummond
did lay down in a rented one room with single bed
and a beat-up desk. We know what happened next.

A LAMENT FOR MARGARITA MAHFOUZ

Weep all you lovers for Margarita Mahfouz
our own local beauty deserving star turn
up on the silver screen, marquee dazzling
like Dorothy Dandridge.

Lament, devotees of art and beauty
for an artiste who rolled
with belly dancers east side
at Club Havana.
In the days before
Nettleford's national
dance theatre.

O Companeros, consider if our sister
had jetted that ninety miles to Cuba
and performed at the Tropicana,
and Fidel had found her.
But this picture shows her in limbo
slipping below the bar.

Iyata Jah daughter, kings would cast down
crowns for; is gone. Here was lionheart gal
turned sacrificial lamb, bad love cut short
her heart message song.

She and her three sisters would gaze up at the seven others
and detect big Orion in his blinged-out belt on night patrol
with sword and dog, on guard against rogue meteors.

In those open-air cinemas that we had on these islands then:
roofless, no rain, stars above, stars ahead on the screen,
and Margarita star-struck, close-marked their movements.

Convinced that with luck she'd be star of screen and stage
for she was hotter than Ginger Rogers by half, and she'd be
better cast than Judy Garland as sultry Minnie from Trinidad.

She had Arab blood enough to play Rider Haggard's *She*,
the immortal Ayesha Queen of Kor, awaiting reincarnation
of her murdered mortal lover. She lived under a volcano.

And Don was in the audience also taking note of the style
of horn-playing men who carried the swing, in musicals
set at the Copa, the Tropicana and the Mocambo.

He was star boy like them, but he flared out into dark hole
when he ventured too far outside his own cosmic system.

GROUNATION

The hemp sash cord that raised and lowered
the window frame snapped as she hoisted it
to thief out when her sisters fell asleep.

No one called her back as she raced toward
Long Mountain range reeled in by force
of chant and drum sound.

She entered the compound through veils
of smoke and incense and joined in
the chorus of lament: Africa we want to go.

What drew her to this company of outcasts
where she burned bright as an altar candle
at this nocturnal rite of dreadness?

Who called her to attend the assembly
of beardface and dreadlocks Rastaman?
Why did she not become one

of the long skirt, all tresses covered,
modest and obedient, trod behind
sistren of downcast eyes?

How did she see herself as she jumped
nyabighi to basso funde and skitter
of kete drum?

When or where, time or date, they first met.
Romantics believe that it happened one night
as he performed with the Skatalites on stage
and she stood there in the wings in waiting.

He sighted her up when he paused, so Dizzy
Moore the trumpeter could solo; Don lowered
his trombone and caught sight of her standing
still in the wings, cool as a marble statue.

Waiting in the wings she'd always go quiet.
None around her able to coax response
from her save silence. She'd look skyward,
slow her heartbeat to near stop, and let

the spotlight mark her place; allow music
to build suspense, made the audience wait
until she was released from standstill into life
again. He saw her at resurrection moment.

A stone nymph who before his gaze broke free
from becalmed state and with a whirlpool
froth of skirts, swirled into his melancholy life.
She entered aiming for the light.

WOMAN A COME (1)

I

Song of herself she composed herself from Rastafari
chant, Hollywood musicals and ancestral memories
of Bedouin airs keened as camel trains near oases.

Song of herself: track cut in the wax of Black Swan,
became her swan song, her one and only song
to the Divine through her Ungu Malungu Man.

We hear her speech before her song; her shy self-
introduction girlish is: Iyata Jah daughter, woman
a come, before she hits a high key and sings it slant.

Her heart message: she wants us to give it to him
should we see him before her; she has no desire
to live without him, this king of ace from kingdom

in outer space, only other occupant of their private
planet Venturian. Where when she is in her solitude,
she hears, she says, she hears, not imaginary sounds

but sweet melodies, of her beautiful Ungu Malungu man.

II

This comely granddaughter of Lebanon, flamboyant
in frilled, flounced costume she designed herself
slashed and ribboned by a killing blade.

For she broadcasted the private name she moaned
to a demi-god who ate clay as he stargazed.
The knock-softly one who concealed all trace

of that border place where two half-angels coupled
on the uncharted planet, Venturian

III

His lips that gave music to spirit vibrations
most times unuttered by mortals, could not give
shape nor sound to her wild woman chanson.

He could not bear to see her arrange her limbs
in arabesques for hot-breath crowds; his complaint
called for her to perform for him and him alone.

For his legions of demons stood down when she raised
high the banner of love, she salved him with amber
honey, she was cure-all, she was his medicine.

We all know how it went down. Peace be on them now.

WOMAN A COME (2)

Woman a come with selfless love
her fragrant body repurposed
as bleeding beating bag.

Flag woman in the band of women
who love strong, heat seeker of warrior
mettle equal to her own.

Lover with bottle enough to believe
all-heal streamed from her pores
in waves sufficient to buoy an angel

fallen from head place in the seraphs's
horn section. What of her children?
She loved them. She left them!
No, he took them.
She lost them.

THE DARK DESTROYER

O the multiple ways
that boxer made her bleed.

Some of these she listed
on November 21 Nineteen Sixty Four
when she appeared before a judge
in Sutton Street Divorce Court.

She'd come seeking access
to her children he'd taken
away to British Honduras.

He chopped, kicked, punched her
and blacked both her eyes.

Wrapped her long hair round
his knuckles like a sleek glove
then hurled her to the curb
and flung the baby after her.

It took four strong men
to lift him off her
when he pressed down
on her face with a pillow.

He ripped off her clothes.
She tore up Slipdock Road
clad in shreds of nightgown.

One deft blow
was delivered full force
to the side of her neck
with the edge of his hand
like an axe.

He was in the hurt business.
Billed as 'The Dark Destroyer'
one of the world's prize fighters.
Soaking wet she weighed in
at maybe 110 lbs.

NIGHT RESCUE

She pictured them wilding like Mowgli in Jungle Book,
in a far place where Indians—the ones Jamaicans
used to call Arawaks—still live.

Indians and descendants of Africans who grow logwood
in thickets; from it they are skilled at extract and brew
of a liquid that holds fast the colour black.

Dye fix they call that. Her husband's people are capable
of making what is dark stand fast, and in still of night
he came and captured her children,

the man-made law of the land insist are his by right.
He has rowed them across muddy waters to bush place
where sulphur-eyed jaguars stalk, and waterfalls drown

the eyewater of her children bawling for Mama Margarita.
In the yard where hardwood trees host bruise-coloured
orchids, his mother informs them, 'Your mother dead'.

Above the harridan screech of Macaws, Margarita calls
'My babies, your mother is coming' as she swings vine
to vine like Hollywood actresses do in Tarzan movies

she'd take in with her sisters on Saturdays at the Palace.
She wakes exhausted; bedsheets twisted to rope,
from futile night effort to fetch her little ones home.

So she turns and pours the kindness milk she cannot feed
her children, on to one man wounded beyond cure,
who will one New Year's morning take her life…

Because, she dance half naked.
Because, she give him him medicine late.
Because, he said, she stab herself.

TESTIMONY OF A FRIEND

You think I never see you when you jump over the wall
Desmond Dekker

Even if she did see you when you jump over the wall,
when you accidentally fall and expose your holey
holey drawers, and you pop you bitter gall,
and yes, you crying now fi ice water.

She would keep your secret lock tight like the lid
of the enamel pail where you soak soap and rinse
you stain-up small clothes you leave overnight
to moon-bleach on a sheet of sun-hot zinc.

O if she was your friend.

Of all the ninety and nine, the name she prized most
was The Friend. And if you and her got along,
and if you and her spirit take. If you were her bona fide
you could not want a better confidante.

And yes, she was fiery, O yes she would fight you,
but she'd help you to take the fight to your demons.
She was Don's one true friend. She gave her life to him.
Now she is the slandered saint of hard-love women.

TESTIMONY OF HER RASTA BRETHREN

Her aspect and appearance was like that of a queen,
she was one of the fairest damsels in East Kingston.
And if riches were what her heart's desire had been
it would be easy for her to catch any big money man
on this island, and then turn round and look down
on we who grow up with her in Kingston 2.

But she was what we call well grounds: she identify
with the rebel spirit of Rastafari; she did not abandon
the brethren even when Babylon did designate I
and I inhuman. And when Vere Johns knock we aside
and declare that there was no opportunity for Rasta
to perform on that stage,

she, who the crowd come to see, said, If my Brethren
can't go on, I refuse to perform—and she was headline
and star attraction. So it was that night became the hour
the public came to hear what we had been preparing
behind smoke screen for years. Yes, it was Margarita
who opened the way for the Mystic Revelation.

When the news of the coming of the prophet
fell not on stony hill, but back O wall,
we the descendants of captured Africans set up
camp in the East and kept vigil awaiting news
of the arrival of our soon coming King.

Night and day we send up smoke signals
to flight of spirit mesenjahs; determined
that the time of arrival should reach us first:
O spirit when u reach when you hover over
Palisadoes follow the scent of green iscence

bear right on approaching Rockfort.
For we are waiting in Wareika hills, where we
can be located by sound of chant and drum.
One thousand four hundred and ninety feet high
is this hill named for our Black skin Maori brethren,

also down under Babylonian system; we wait
in Wareika in the foothills of Long Mountain.
From where we'll march in our tens of thousands
come from all corners of this island, we forward
to meet our rightful King. Confirming spirit

till you come we will hold this beat; we reject
Babylonish riddim into which we cannot fit.
And our sistren Margarita and I idren Don
are with us as spirit members of our tribe.
Tribe of the Earth's Most Strangest Ones.

ON THE DAY TEACHER GAVE I THIS AS A SONG TO SING

Ging gang goolie goolie wash wash—Wash what?
ging gang go, ging gang go—   Where must ging's gang go?
Aallo, aallo, shello, aallo shello—   Yellow shell O, shell of yellow
Shally wally shally wally—   Shall Wally, what shall Wally wash?

Ging gang goolie goolie wash wash ging gang go ging gang go.

Me and my gang—or my ging—know it was time to go.

Go and stretch the skin of the sacrificial goat round the hoop
of iron, to contain, then relay the beat that give us livity.
In ship's hold, I told my sistren: I do not want to die as stolen one.
Wash wash this: I and I heart-beat is how I live to keep Count

Ossie and the players of instruments pass through the gates
of the government school and cast-off colonial khaki clothes
for coarse garments of crocus; shoeless or slampatta shod
one by one they paid final courtesy call to the Barbershop

to contribute comb, brush, black and white Pluko hair oil
and sheep fat lanolin pomade, to form fuel for funeral pyre
that send up smoke signals and signs: Now is the time
of the opening of the locks, the allowing of the knots.

O mother don't you weep for I and I

No more will I comb the streets of Babylon.
No more will I desire them not to give I the brush off.
No more will I and I wait in vain without the gates.
No more will I grease the palms of gatekeepers
who cannot themselves enter within, to let I and I in.

O mothers of Jamaica Weep not for your daughters
O mothers from henceforth we will be Queens.
No mother, we no longer aspire to enter Miss Jamaica
beauty contest our complexion will not ever win.

Contest meant for near white weepdroppers to win.
White in their own eyes till they go to foreign,
and find out what a disqualifier their wee drop
of black blood is. It is then they come back.
Blacker than black: Blackness retroactive.

How beautiful on Long Mountain are thy feet
O sistren
Your slender feet in leather sandals crafted
by your kingman; skilled in leathercraft I am.
Your red green and gold garments fragrant with iscence.
Your lioness locks beneath crown you yourself knit.

We are the craftsmen and women of Rastafari.
We hold no interest in babylonish merchandise.
We are arbiters of our own roots fashion and style
that one day the whole world will follow behind.

O Babylon, our designs are inspired by embrace
of everything about I and I that you do not rate.
From crown of our heads to soles of our feet
I and I am I own original aesthete.

We fly our knotty locks which have always
been rough and offensive to your eye.
We firebun all hot comb, refuse all lye.
Instead of straight, we knot. We locks.

We elevate it in the coconut tree style
of Steel Pulse King David Hinds.
We low it make it leggo down to ground.
We locks long like Junior Gong.

Bald it sometime. For we come to find
there is many a righteous baldhead Rastafari.

We are the craftsmen and women of Rastafari.
We hold no interest in babylonish merchandise.
We are arbiters of our own roots fashion and style
that one day the whole world will follow behind.

By yon bonny banks of gully bank
there we'll dwell in naturality.
By yon bonnie braes of open-air
university, where the curriculum
offers Reasoning 101:

How to call down lightning
thunder and brimstone
following the fashion
of prophets of old.

How to practice Health Science
that is: carminative expulsion
from brain, blood and intestine
of all babylonish self hatred.

How to reinstate Bungo Natty
to great, via ancient
routes of repatriation
to the motherland,
even as we trod the path
of upfullness
and reject the route of swine.

How to step across creation
regarding all things living
with the I of peace and love,
therefore we kill and eat
no flesh.
Ital is what
our way is.
Ital—what you now
call plant based.

The time has come
—must and bound to come—
when the system same one
will fall in step with
our before it time
green movement.

Movement of Peace and Love.
Peace and Love I leave with you.
Peace and Love.

Twenty-one thousand miles we have come to see the king.
Our hopes and dreams arrived in advance on the Black Star Line;
Marcus Garvey, our captain and guide through dark night.

I and I Douglas Mack, Philmore Alvaranga and Mortimo Planno
are three who sighted your star in the east as we kept vigil
awaiting the crowning of our Black king.

And we have come, O King, bearing gifts:

Ras Alvaranga:
I present your majesty with this box carved from lignum Vitae
upon the lid is etched the continent of Mother Africa with you
O emperor, holding your corner in Ethiopia.

Ras Douglas Mack:
Accept, your highness this painting done in the verdant green
shades of the parish of Portland; it is of Navy Island, owned
by a star boy by the name of Errol Flynn.

One man own a island, and we the descendants of stolen Africans
are forced to kotch on the eyelid of gully bank and capture land,
off which we are hunted down like wild animal.

Accept Negus, this woolen representation of our own banner
—Red green and gold—knitted together by the skilled hands
of Ras Mortimo Planno.

One more thing we bring:

This photograph of a weeping widow woman, she is surrounded
by her fatherless children; her kingman cut down by Babylon.
This picture show our own condition.

And the eyes of the emperor that can see far, fill to the brim.
Reflected in them are his massive black-maned palace lions,
themselves reflected in the gaze of the three dreads.

LALIBELA

in Memoriam Ras Makonnen

The hour he was being called home
he made a vow to take her as bride again
when they are reunited in Lalibela.
She will be robed in wedding garments
with bands of red green and gold;
her flesh will be cooled from her bath
in Ethiopia's Jordan River.

In a tall underground church hewn
from rock by skilled Ethiopians,
in the same era that Europeans
raised up cathedrals, Jah Makonnen
will again take the hand of his Queen.

Done with the way of the outcast.
Done with bun down Babylon.
For Babylon will burn on its own
if it change not, up from low and carnal
into natural, upfull, compassionate.

At the last, before leaving earth plain
Ras Makonnen said unto his beloved:
Do not weep; I go before you my queen
to Lalibela, to prepare our wedding feast.

SHASHEMANE

Let the wanderer take the long way
home to Ithaca; and John receive
his revelations in fever dreams
on his isle of Patmos.

My friend Hopey's face is set
towards Shashemane, in Ethiopia.

For when I reach Shashemane,
Hopey says, on the day
my plane touch down
I will kneel and kiss the ground.
I will feel at last, at home.

Since I sight up I am no
longer at ease among these
people in this alien land
where everything
about my skin and self
is an offense.

I will arise and go now
to Shashamane
where I will run
unhemmed by boundary
and wire fence.
There will be no rockstone
to buck my big toe on,
no police macca
to draw blood from
my foot bottom.

Our holy land in Ethiopia
given us by His Majesty's hands.

There the lion-heart
will lie down alongside
the woolly lambs,
under own fig tree and vine.

O what a day of rejoicing,
when I and I reach Shashemane.

HIE YOU AWAY FROM THAT NUNNERY

after Isabella and the Pot of Basil

This is set in a convent where a nun
who had been living for seven years as a bride
of Christ because she thought a holy life would
anneal her broken heart, one day received a letter
by the hand of the nunnery's ancient watchman.
The missive said that her true love who had
been forced to marry a woman he had gotten
with child (which was what had caused the nun
to leave the world behind) was now divorced.
She tried not to rejoice (overmuch) but sent in return,
assurance that her love for him still lived. Messages
flew back and forth between them. In truth they did not
fly, but were passed back and forth by the beady-eyed
greased-palm, bribe-taking watchperson,
who conspired with them to make arrangements.
'There is a bell, a bell that ring every early morning'
the watchie told her love newly uncoupled, 'when you
hear that bell be sure you are waiting outside'.
So that dawn when the bells pealed for the service
of lauds, and the line of holy sisters walked to mass
by Kyrie Eleison of bird chant, and sweet scent
of basil set in clay pots lined the straight path,
the young nun stopped all of a sudden, so abrupt,
that the old sister walking behind her with eyes shut
telling her beads fervently, all but fell down on her face.
The young nun suddenly stepped out of her place,
and spun round in a circle, as she peeled off
her tall headdress. Her hands pulled at the rope cord
anchoring her wimple, she ripped at the wafer-like
breastplate shielding her breasts, dropped it in the grass
at her feet and bolted through gates that opened out
to let her into the arms of her worldly love.

HOUSEWIFE'S CHOICE

for Dennis Scott

She was rattling her cage, plotting escape.
She'd sharpened a sawtooth knife to saw through
the wrought iron rails.

Same knife she used to limb from limb a chicken
she simmered in red wine, thyme and bay leaf
and served up in tureen at a dinner party.

When Dennis appeared in her doorway and said:
'Whatever else you let go of, you must hold on
to Poetry; it has been sent to save you.'

She should have invited him in to sit and partake
of that fancy coq au vin prepared for people
whose faces she cannot now remember.

She should have chucked those froggish padlocks
securing the lips of the wrought iron grill gate
into the swimming pool.

She should have bolted to the bus depot and caught
the Portland flyer, she should have quit that life
earlier, but she waited till she read her own

teacup and the tea leaves revealed there was
not one leaf of love remaining in that house,
and if she didn't run, her head would.

SISTER IGGY AND MARGARITA CROSS OVER TO THE FIELD OF THE LAMENTS

The mulatto ferryman said, you two Jamaican women
have paid enough, keep your coins, I'll row you across
to the spot from where you can walk to the new green
field, where the ones who love without reserve gather.

A Lament sister, Love's caretaker, stands there tall
as a lighthouse; she signals to them by flashing her pearls.
They disembark, she stretches out a long arm and helps
them from the shores of rockbottom into the pasture

where the clean stream of wash O washaway sorrows
runs and invites all newcomers to partake of its mineral
waters. Like school girls on a fun day, Margarita and Iggy
wade in, they lift high the hems of gauze garments.

Iggy turns to Margarita, points to her chest and asks
'How are your wounds these days?' Margarita, bold-faced
as always, does not hesitate to back off her blouse and bare
her breasts. See, she says, 'Scars healed and polished'

Sister Ignatius glances sideways: 'Girl cover up yourself,
you're not in the night club now!' They laugh out loud.
Says Iggy, 'O Anita, Blessed mother has answered
my prayers to renew you spirit body mind and soul.

Margarita hugs her. Says, 'thanks Sister', turns and asks
the attendant Lament 'Will Malungu ever be allowed in here?'
Lament: That is not for me to say, but you just be still now,
you might hear strains of 'Snowboy' up in the spheres.

OLD PHOTOGRAPHS FROM MOTHER

Mother slips a snapshot under your door: a black and white image
of a younger girl wearing your half smile. Fadeaway into dark room.

Is she all gone, the wild woman?

Mother conjures a red clay bird she animates with allspice breath.
It warbles, wings, wheels and comes, in its beak a glossy pimento leaf.

Over the mountain with Dawn, mother comes skylarking, skylarking.
she dives in and clears river of slime stones set to trip up young girls.

Laughter hula hoops bulrushes mother gathers for Moses baby basket.
Kinetic is the frock tail swish, gallivanting is what young gal laughter is.

Next time you see mother she is belly-woman heavy with what must be
One whole infant school. She big. Gravid as August rainclouds she is.

Fatty fatty. Bun in the oven. Mama Tumba.

But as you think you will witness deliverance, she same one dispatches
you on urgent errand, orders you send barrel not to, but from, Jamaica

to school children in a cold storage. Barrel of cornmeal porridge words
to spicen cold breakfast feeding program; and you never get to see

all she was big with. But on your return to open uncurtained room
bright sunlight at midnight reveals: A round table prepared for you—

All fruits ripe and sliced clean to display medallion pinned and pegged
against purple skin, offset by rind-dimpled ortaniques-half orange.

I leave these for you, her copperplate join-up states, picked them myself, washed them clean, arranged them in the blue dish by the brass vase

haphazard with sundry country flowers.

She never leaves. Come, go, arrival, departure, in season she allows you glimpses of her honing your craft: captions of sepia photographs.

BUSHA'S WOMAN

She recalls an ancestral blessing for long life:
'May you live till them sun you'.
As she spreads weftless sheets on shale
rocks to dry, her own skin wrinkles.

The end-of-year northers fissure and crack
the walls of her wattle and daub house.
O damp and rheums. Duppy umbrellas bloom
under floorboards, the loose thatch roof leaks.

Her flesh, weary of holding on, hammocks
and slackens from stomach and breasts.
Her light complexion that caused busha
to single her out when she was but slip of a girl

dims. He promised her a concrete nog house
with wrought iron gate and padlock. Promised
to send for her by end of August 1838. She waits.
Other women can be so cruel.

Such taunt songs they sing as they go pass, laugh
and cut eye, cut eye to slice her down to level.
Pretend friends and ceitful ones always inquire,
'So when last you hear from Busha?

the Last to Be Set Free

I tell my friend Quasheba, stop up you ears with this beeswax,
so that the bantering song of all the one who leave scotch free
don't mad we who still bind to cane piece. We who get left back
because spiteful Massa say: 'Emancipation is like an aged white
rum—so strong not every Negro can imbibe at one time, lest they
grow drunken and stagger'. So him water down freedom, share
it out little little and what left in a barrel bottom is fi me and you.

I say, Don't bawl Q, we wait long already, we can wait more still.
She say: 'Since them carry me come from Guinea me want go home.'
Me too. But if is one thing me learn from what Saint Paul preach
is: They that wait. No, is not him say that, must be the prophet
Isaiah or one other man who help write Massa bible with the lock
and key. My friend say she don't want hear no comfortable words
today. My heart string stretch out too. Me disappoint. Me tired pray.

Bend down! Full-free hurrycomeup dem a come down the road
like a Syrian wolf upon the fold. I no rightly sure what that mean,
but me like how it sound. Turn you back and bend down lower,
inspect grass hard like a cruel overseer. Bend down, chop furious
and cuss like wicked slave driver. Tell grass how it good-fi-nothing,
lazy, and no make fi flourish. Say it bad like sin that Ham commit.
Them gone? We can stand up now. Our day of Jubilee a come.

ADDRESS TO THE WEED IN THE CANE PIECE

Pretty little grass weed, to me you are a sweet rose,
even though some don't think so. According to them,
it matters not that you bud and blossom, you do not
count as flowers, therefore you not good enough
to cut and put in a water vase and set pon table
in a big house. So them order me, a human weed,
to dig you down, and root you up, and fling you
to one side, although your roots bind the ground
together. You're as good as any other growing thing,
you are just planted where you're less counted.
To me little weed you are sweet as any roses.

QUASHEBA'S LAMENT

I know how to abase, I know how
to abound. How to press my big toe
aground, and bite my tongue.

I taste my own salt blood
and remind myself I am still alive
and there is hope while there is life.

I knot up my belongings in my bundle;
dem send and say is not my time yet.
I loosen the knot and I wait.

I calculate the silver money I save up
in a shutpan under my house-bottom
for the day my day of freedom come.

And every day I bend down and draw
in the dirt, O Jesus, I draw a straight
line that lead to freedom come.

I draw my own house with a front door.
I forge my lock and key. I turn the key.
I lock me inside until such time as I leave.

LAST WORDS

Yes, is true. Some who get freedom first
pass and mock the first of August Nayga
the last to get emancipation. Yes sir.

We had was to bear all the commotion
and bangarang of old pan as them galang
past we out a the estate.

Some believe the foolishness the hard heart
say bout freedom not for any and every one.
How some need to be

led with bridle and bit like mule and horse.
Not because some get let go first,
always remember this:

It matters not when you did leave.
Every single one a we
come out a the cane piece.

LAMENT OF THE WEE-DROPPERS

As the West India regiment decamped,
a band of wee-droppers congregated
keening in the rain outside Duppy gate.

These ladies made moan and called after
departing lorries: O do not, do not forget
we the fair Jamaican girls

you romanced at those Saturday night
soirees at Up park Camp; under the argent
Jamaican moon, we silver spooned.

And you pledged that you'd take us home
to motherland there to meet your Mam
and Da in some shire of England.

You promised as you took us to camp beds,
but now you are departed, where O where
will we find suitable husbands?

We'll have to make alliances with itinerant
foreigners going native, be rejected by Aid
workers who like girls thick—dark as molasses.

We'll have to flee to source spouses in Europe.
We will never speak of what occurred there
in Europe. We'll just return to local shores

and rent-a-dread.

We who sat out Black is Beautiful, appalled
by independent tie-head sufferers and God
forbid, a black prime minister!

Will have to be counted with the common
herd. We will perforce have to acknowledge
our more than just a wee drop of black blood.

MANY NATIVE WOMEN MISSING

At first it seemed
it was just
the cedar tree
extending a limb
to one or two
disembodied
red dresses
but now the forest
is redolent
with wind-sock
frocks twisting
from branches
of firs, pines
and arbutus.
The shadow
of a black mother
bear climbs up
unto warning posters
tears at the hems
of empty dresses.
Scores of Native
women missing.

QUILT

This lady has asked me to record that no one less than Saint Anne,
patron Saint of seamstresses, appeared in a vision and handed her
a big-eyed golden needle, a spool of silver thread, and commanded
her to stitch a quilt for Missus Queen herself.

And I think how since I quit the estate all l sleep on is cold ground
with rockstone pillow under my head. I think to myself how a scribe
like me could use a quilt to fold and function as rug when I prostrate
myself; one I could roll as a bolster for my neck,

when I sit under a tree to meditate and receive inspiration from leafy
ancestral spirits. I would take care of it. Wash it. Shield it from scorch
stare of hot sun so it would not fade out. Darn it when I rip it, save it
for the day I can broad-off like missus

across my feather bed. One day, one day I will purchase a feather bed.
You don't believe me? You wait and see. Be that as it may, I almost said
when this lady approached me and requested that I write her story
for she is not strong in the literacy department—

this lady who appears to me like she's bound for Newcastle with a load
of excess coal—I am certain her Highness is not short of fine bed linen
and such delights up there in her royal mansion that is grander by far
than any Jamaican great house.

She surely hath quilts of silver and gold; embossed, festooned, inlaid,
arrayed with precious stones; what would she want with your humble
local needlework? But a still small voice said, what if this woman
really believes that Charity never faileth?

What if Saint Anne, really did appeareth? and sayeth she is to maketh
a thing of beauty to be a joy forever to a queen? A thing to cut a dash
across her gold post most splendiferous bed—Bless the many millions
from the Gold Coast whose labour produced that wagga wagga.

So I say to her, I will record for posterity how you skillfully joined up
all manner of leftover cotton, second-hand silk and satin, nappy velvet,
and piece-a-piece of all and sundry fabric, and unite them into two quilts
for which you will receive abundant Blessings in return.

And having committed this to paper, the payment I ask for now I'm done
is that you give me, your womanmanuensis, one.

THIS PASTEL ON PAPER LAID ON ALUMINIUM PORTRAIT SHOWS

Germaine Greer dressed up in a red Jean Muir dress,
battered old-gold lace-up oxfords, knees set wide,
head tilted left, hands roped and rough.

And she was sitting down just so on that night in 1972
when my sister and me went to her talk in Kingston.
We all could see how tall she was even when sitting down—

We watched her stride on stage like she owned the place,
all but straddle her chair and arranged for her long legs
never to meet : Like her knee dem a keep malice!

And then she lap her frock tail like a market woman
and started in: she proceeded to school the scandalized
audience. Said we Jamaican women should demand

the government set up free abortion clinics and provide
us with free childcare services so we'd be better feminists.
Cue claat and outrage from men in the audience.

We loved it! But for me the night's high point took place
when she described with great respect, a meeting
she'd had with rape victims in Bangladesh.

And how these women had shown her a medicine plant
the stem of which they'd insert inside themselves
to prevent pregnancy after rape.

And that is my treasured takeaway from Ms Greer's talk.
I would like to ask my sister what she remembers
and that thought brings tears.

Ah, sister Germaine, I was proud of how you then seemed
to respect the way many of us third world women
negotiate hard life.

But did you really refer to Aboriginal Australians
as spear chuckers? and why go so hard to exclude
what you regard as non-native plants from your yard?

MAIDEN'S BLOOD ENERGY DRINKS

On Mount Alban
prepubescent
Zapotec girls picked
as living offerings
laid flat
on stone altars.

Jeweled daggers
hilted to left breast
release caged
red bird hearts
to appease wrath
of cantankerous gods
who crank handle
moon and sun machines.

Do parched old deities need
maiden's blood
energy drinks?
Must craven old deities
lust to ingest
the mysterious
of women's bodies?

BRING BACK OUR GIRLS

I

Memo to the world.
Entire armies have not managed
to spring all our stolen schoolgirls
from that pack of barking mad rass
wicked and dreadful loco haram.
To remind you, a snapshot:

In this picture we see them swathed
in coarse-cloth rough regulation burqas.
One girl cradles a baby in her arms.
We hear they've been given
as child brides to murderers.
We hear they are being groomed
to be suicide bombers.

We can see for ourselves how they seem
adrift. Small frail vessels at sea.
Or out-of-focus graduation group portrait
from bad luck's let them down academy.

II

Standing on Harbour Street with the mother
of the missing girl, as we look out to sea
she says we should search all those ships
before we make them leave, for they are
taking our children away in those same
ships you see there. How I know this?
It's because nobody ever bless eyes on
them again anywhere on this island.
Standing with the mothers of the missing.

TALITHA CUMI

She is not dead, but sleeping.
Little girl I say unto you arise.
Talitha Cumi

For none will keen of your gone too soon.
Not for you the Aha! so we would have it.
Talitha Cumi

Your story will not be crooned
by watermouth rumheads as
the song of the drunkards at the gates.

Babygirl your fate will not be their musick.
Give praise to just in time save.
Talitha Cumi

Still you should know
professional mourners will be enraged
when you are raised from the dead

Talitha Cumi. Talitha Cumi.

They'll feel robbed, deprived of freeness
funeral food chewed as they dryweep
over your loss, your loss.

Even as corpses lie there
unburied in their own house.

OUR LADY MARION ANDERSON

Entered and left by these steps that serve
as stage on which you and your son stand
and wait for your lift at evening time.

Evening Time: hymn of ease after beatdown
hammer of hot sun; sweet air sung for her
when she requested we sing her one of our own.

The D.A.R scorned our lady Marion
till good Eleanor walked her to the capitol steps.

Our Lady Marion:

'Prejudice is like a hair across your cheek,
you can't see it, you can feel it
you keep brushing at it.'

And her laments raise up ramshackle.
And her praise seals shatter of hearts.
And times such as these times call
for Anthems. Anthems like hers.

ADVERT FOR MAHALIA'S SINGING

Armies of darkness hard
hard on your heels,
determined you should not enter
the promised Promised Land?

Rally under Mahalia's banner.

Your head a haunted house?
her keys can tumble back
rusty locks on iron bars of fear O.

Spite spirits outside wisdom's door
who cannot enter in themselves,
yet bar the way to prevent you?

Her cut and clear melody
runs them through.

Digged pits? Her singing fills.
Traps set? Her chant exposes.

You're guaranteed to look back in wonder
when she commands interfering spirits:
'Stand There.'

Stand there till you drop.
Drop and become door stop
used to kotch wisdom's door open.

Mahalia: 'I did some work for the Lord this evening!'

FOR SANDRA BLAND

O Sandra Bland was cast in a low budget
remake of mean streets, as lone woman driver
who spots a cop car in her rearview mirror
and in panic crosses the thin white line.

Blue uniform in a rage swears she did not indicate.
Fires orders for her to put out her cigarette.
She goes off script; told him it was her car,
she was entitled to smoke in it if she wanted.

The camera captures her flung to the curb.
She is restrained and locked down in a jail cell.
On the third day she rises hanged by the neck,
her feet pressing at the last on air brakes.

A critic on Fox writes her off, gives her thumbs down
for acting all arrogant; for not taking directions.
For her part, all she did was leave home, drive her car
and change lanes. Say her name.

SAY SOMETHING FOR ME ENGLISH?

for Paulette Wilson and Amelia Gentleman

This is what the market women call after her in Mandeville
Market. Say something. Anything, then say, innit?
We love how you talk sweet.

Like how you say, 'That coco, its a commander coco, innit?'

These days she does not tarry long among the market women.
She does not pause at their stalls to run jokes and banter
with them about their prices, dearer than Brixton market.

She does not scold how she can buy three pounds of yellow yam
in England, for the price of the one they are trying to sell her.
'And you blighters grow the yam right here, innit?'

Gwan, they say, you too mean, open you English leather purse
and release some a dem strong English pound you have
under lockdown.

What happen English me think you gone back by now!

Home. Her thoughts had floated on the clouds cushioning
the airplane down to soft landing. Home to her kitchen
where her red kettle waited to whistle a home coming.

First thing she'd planned to do when she'd set her suitcase
 down after entering into her own house purchased
with money saved from forty years of factory work

was brew herself a cuppa. She could almost taste her coming
home cup of tea, the exact same blend that tastes altogether
different on the tongue when she brewed it in Jamaica.

Something to do with alkalinity, difference in the waters.
Sixty years she has lived in the motherland.
Arrived there with her mother and father as a babe in arms.

When they told her upon arrival that what she travelled on
is not a real British passport, they said they'll be needing
proof she's really been living there for sixty years.

Crazy amounts of receipts from every place she's lived
in Britain and no NHS. No form of benefits, till all is settled...
She's back in Mandeville. She pretends it is where she wants to be.

She no longer laughs and jokes when the market women say,
'Say something for me nuh, English?

Last night she saw another Windrush victim on TV who said
he and his family decided that if he was deported, he'd carry
enough sleeping pills with him to end it.

Say something for me nuh English?

A WOMAN LIKE YOU

Two women who hitch outside Trail Bay mall call to me
as I breeze across Cowrie street; 'Hey Sister, what you
doing in these parts?' I drift over and join them.

Like me they're no longer young, just not yet past it.
Think trio of ripened hipsters going soft pear shaped;
green at core and heart.

I hover like a hummingbird become icon in re-set
of my style—Think West Coast-West Indian between
two wide seas: Salish and Caribbean.

Aren't you going to tell us where you're from?

Jamaica. We Love Jamaica! Loud laugh, start chant
stir up, stir up Marley and Toots. Needs must, I join
in the rub a dub on the sidewalk.

Then a pause. One says, You should come with us.
Where would you take me? She says, I know people,
who would really love a woman like you.

The wild woman is not all gone; she still shows
herself when her kind appear, running hard.

LIONESS

It is Sunday and we are off to the Lion park,
but first we must pass this parade of ostriches:
mother and father and a float of small babies

with fabulous plumage still in tufty stage, soft
furze that will in time feather into ostentations
ladies used to die for to decorate their hats.

This parade causes the car to slow at the crossing
sign that warns: Beware of smaller animals.
Parents taking children to bush Sunday school?

Thule gears down and we observe the birds: a lark
thrilla on a thorn bush, and to welcome me back
the blacksmith plover strikes up.

The lion enclosure gates are guarded by a young woman
you ask if she is afraid, Wonder Girl says, no, never.
Look behind her. Right there all golden and large,

nothing between us but razor wire fence and metal gate
Miss lion-heart operates, there in your line of sight,
seated sphinx-like, cross-wise the dusty trail, is a lioness.

No zoo beast this. In her element she is magnificence.
That head; even with tresses relinquished to flash locks
of man-lion, even so, that low afro head cropped close,

is its own planet. A sizable sun set on a turmeric
powdered body. We pull up alongside the fence, we read
the sign, we do all it says, this makes sense.

There have been incidents. There is tape. That woman last
year who thought she'd film a lion up close because it was
lazing all at ease and Disney; till it lifted up and there is no

stopwatch to clock the speed which cut the distance
between woman and lion. We wind the windows
all the way up. The lioness lolls in a beauty queen pose.

Done win already; Miss honey, sweet-biscuit, amber
and pollen. For her, Joburg's mines have been stripped.
This lion queen never deigns to roar, she just shows

full set of teeth as she half rotates her massive world
head set there a golden globe on her strong stem neck.
That is all that's needed, that is her 'don't even test'.

We gaze at her majestic under her own sign, the sun
applying more gold streaks and highlights to her pelt.

CHRISTMAS MARKET

24 December 2020

And if it could just be Christmas Eve again,
when I was small; and the evening air was all
redolent, with the pepper reek of clappers,
mingling with nutmeg, cinnamon, and clove,
scent of currants and raisins in rum for a year.

And me and my siblings and friends, dressed up
in our brand new Christmas dan-dan, all excited
to galang down town to visit Christmas market.
And stars would stream out from sticks, like lit-up
sceptres held aloft, and everyone had on a crown

of crepe paper, printed with some festive slogan
like: Mary's Boy Child is born; O What a La La Pon
the Beebop! Just Kiss Me quick! As we make merry
in Christmas Market, where our finest craftsmen
and women come from near and far to set up stall.

Such wonders on offer: Marvellous toys for delight
of little pickney: see miniature wheeled vehicles,
fabricated from wood, rubber, zinc and anything
that one could turn hand to fashion into plaything,
then coat with bright shade of house paint enamel.

And carved and painted animals enough to fill a stable.
From the gentler fires of iron monger manufacturer
—Son of Ogun—come mini coal pot stoves; and cute pots,
large enough to cook a meal to fill a dolly's mouth.
The first furniture I owned was bought for me one

Christmas, from the stall of a carpenter named Mr Joseph.
A royal blue table and two chairs: one yellow, one purple.
I make myself little again and sit down at it to write this:
May we return one day soon to better days. In my mind,
in the purple chair, at that level blue table, I invite you
to sit across from me in the throne of a gold yellow seat,
to speak of days gone by, and pray and wish, for advent,
of beneficent ones to come. And we'll laugh long and loud,
and share well wishes, like slices of rich black Christmas
pudding; and raise toast after toast, with tumblers of wine
red sorrel. Here's to your good health, my dearly beloved,
I have missed you. I miss you so tell. Mi brother,
mi sister, fren good fren, may we no more be strangers.

And the night will resound jubilant with noise of fee-fee,
shak-shak, and bands of toy drums. Lo Christmas comes
on clouds descending, in pink miraculous cotton candy,
purchased with shine willy pennies, and feasted on.
On our Christmas Eve walkbout, round and round Parade

to King street, by twinkle of starlight when no child sleep.

FOR NIGEL

My baby brother could have been taken
for one of those cherubic presences
hovering over the action in a nativity
scene. I stood by his crib and marvelled,
and could not find it in my small self
to be jealous that he'd come to displace
me as the last baby of the family.
I sensed he'd brought something
of the divine into our ordinary lives.
For then came the dreadful day,
when his small chest ceased to work
and his face took on a bluish cast.
My mother bent and put her lips to his
and tried to blow life back into him.
He remained unmoving.

Here entered our neighbour
Midwife Lindsay, who came bearing
basin and ewer like a good woman
in a Vermeer painting. She was all
calm as she streamed hot water
into the wide bowl of white enamel.
Midwife Lindsay held him by the feet,
she dipped him headfirst into hot bath
then into another filled with ice water.
She baptized him back and forth
till he bawled out. She dipped him
till his lungs pumped, he bellowed,
his flesh unmarbled. A miracle.
Everybody said we witnessed a miracle.

GOOD FRIDAY

Mama said we should not abandon Jesus.
That he needed us to stay with him
seeing as how his fairweather disciples

had run away and left him there hanging
on the cross, with only the women—
most of them named Mary—remaining.

Good Friday. The one day of the year
we do not wake to drink hot tea or cocoa;
but some form of lukewarm beverage

to wash down the overnight johnny cakes
we breakfast on. No eggs, no porridge.
Mother does not approach the kitchen;

does not uncover her sewing machine.
She sits in the rocking chair and marks
time by singing from her hymn book.

The radio joins in with all of St Matthew's
Passion, and even the maugre dogs
of Kingston fall silent as we stay still

with our crucified Lord as he suffers.
We do too, until three in the afternoon
when our Lord say: 'It is finished'.

Our mother gathers herself and repairs
to the kitchen. We all cheer as she strikes
the match to start the flame on the stove

to cook our Good Friday meal of fish.
Because some disciples were fishermen?
No, she says , this is not a day for flesh.

ALL SAINTS

I wonder what became of Olwen Gilfillian?
She was my friend in primary school,
and other children said that she and I
we both were inclined to be, 'cry-cry'.

But I think Olwen was even more prone
than me to weep at the littlest thing.
Her eyelids would tremble like moth's
wings, and her big brown eyes

streaked with amber lights like a type
of taw or marble the boys played with,
would brim, and she'd bite her lower
lip and then commence to sobbing.

For what? What you crying for Olwen?
Other children would ask, and she'd just
bawl some more, and sometimes so
she'd not feel alone, I'd cry along with her.

Why you crying Olwen? Maybe she'd say
something like, *Teacher look at me funny,*
and that boy long out him tongue at me,
and that is nasty. And we'd both agree

those were things to make a nine year old
finely tuned girl turn on the waterworks.
I think about Olwen Gilfillian these days
when the world makes me weep.

Specifically, the pandemic makes me weep.
In general, the state of the world. But I hope
Olwen has thrived. I pray she's had a good life.
May her eye-water now fall as tears of joy.

Olwen, if you happen to read this, please
know that I still think of you as my friend
Olwen: named for a princess in a Welsh
folk tale, your name means white footprint.

I weep when I recall how our school
No longer exists. No more All Saints.
Kingston. Jamaica. West Indies.
The world. The world.

ACKNOWLEDGEMENTS

Thanks to Verena Reckord, Herbie Miller and Klive Walker for their brilliant writings on Margarita.

To Sister Carmen Chen See and Cathy Lyn for help with my research on Sister Iggy.

To Dermott Hussey, Garth White, Jerry Small, Julian Jingles, Bunny Goodison, Roy White and Elise Kelly for all they do for our music.

And to my brothers Howard, Kingsley, Karl, Keith and Nigel who brought Jamaican music and musicians into our home from early days.